AN EXOTIC JOURNEY WITH KERALA CUISINES

By

MRS. ALICE JOSE

English Edition

PREFACE

It has been said that "A man should rather have a wife who could cook a good dinner than one who speaks Greek" and that has had been the reason for the origin of this book. The ultimate purpose, though, is to introduce some mouth-watering traditional cuisines of Kerala - 'God's own country'. Kerala cuisine is every food lover's delight. Any food lover cannot wait to try them. In this book, these cuisines offer a multitude of both vegetarian and non-vegetarian dishes ranging from traditional sadya to sea food delicacies and have an abundance of ingredients like coconut, rice as well as spices like cinnamon, clove, and black pepper.

I have tried to present these recipes in a simple and lucid manner so that a debutante can also try them. It is a dream come true for me for getting a platform to pen down my recipes, which is a conglomeration of my experience and my passion for cooking. I am sure these recipes are going to discover the cook inside you.

ACKNOWLEDGEMENT

This book would not have been possible without the enthusiastic help, cooperation and support of my near and dear ones. I thank them from the bottom of my heart. I would like to convey my sincere gratitude to the many people who provided immense help, motivation and support during the penning down of this book. I want to extend my heartfelt thanks to my family who saw me through this book. I would also like to thank everyone who, directly or indirectly, rendered their support towards attaining this goal.

RECIPES

VEGETARIAN

AVIYAL
ELEPHANT YAM DRY ROAST
ERISHERI
FAST TO COOK CURRY
GINGER CURRY
KAALLAN
CHINESE POTATO DRY ROAST
WHITE GOURD CURRY
SPICY PUMPKIN CURRY
DRUMSTICK POTATOCURRY
LEMON CURRY
OLAN
STIR-FRIED YARD LONG BEANS
PULISHERI
SAMBAR
TOMATO GRAVY CURRY
SHALLOT CURRY
POTATO YARD LONG BEANS MASALA CURRY
STIR-FRIED RAW BANANA
RAW BANANA UPPU CURRY
OKRA SAUTÉED WITH COCONUT

CHICKEN

CHICKEN CURRY
CHICKEN DRY ROAST
CHICKEN PICKLE

EGG

EGG ROAST
EGG POTATO CURRY

FISH

PRAWN DRY ROAST
FISH CURRY
FISH PAPPAS
FISH PEERA PATTICHATHU
FISH POLLICHHATHU
FISH THODUCURRY
FISH VATTI PATTICHATHU
SEER FISH SAUTÉED WITH COCONUT
FISH PICKLE

MUTTON

BIRIYANI
CUTLET
MASHED TAPIOCA WITH MUTTON
PEPPER LIVER
MUTTON CURRY
MUTTON CHADACHHATH
MUTTON DRY ROAST

CHUTNEY

COCONUT CHUTNEY
MANGO CHUTNEY
FAST TO COOK CHUTNEY

PICKLE

GREEN CHILI PICKLE
RAW MANGO MUSTARD PICKLE
LEMON PICKLE
GOOSEBERRY PICKLE
RAW MANGO CARROT PICKLE
LEMON WHITE PICKLE

SNACKS

CAKE
VATTAYAPPAM

AVIYAL

Ingredients

1.	Elephant Yam (cubed)	-	1 small cup
2.	White gourd (cubed)	-	1 small cup
3.	Raw banana (chopped lengthwise)	-	1
4.	Drumsticks (cut lengthwise)	-	2
5.	Onion (chopped)	-	1
6.	Green chilies (slit)	-	4
7.	Tomato (chopped)	-	1
8.	Yard long beans, ivy gourd (cut lengthwise)	-	½ cup
9.	Bottle gourd (chopped lengthwise)	-	½ cup
10.	Shallots	-	½ cup
11.	Sour Curd	-	½ cup
12.	Coconut oil	-	2 large spoons
13.	Curry leaves	-	2 sprigs
14.	Red chili powder	-	1 tsp
15.	Turmeric powder	-	1 tsp
16.	Salt, water	-	as required
17.	Coconut (grated)	-	1 half
18.	Garlic cloves	-	4
19.	Cumin	-	¼ tsp

Cook ingredients1, 2, 5, 6 in a cup of water. Once half cooked, add ingredients 4, 8, 9 and let it boil. Add ingredients 3, 7 and cook further. Add red chili powder, turmeric powder and salt into the vegetables, mix and cook. Now add the ground coconut mixture (first grind cumin and garlic well and then add grated coconut and grind to a coarse consistency).Pound shallots and curry leaves in a mortar and add into the vegetable mixture. Mix well. Once cooked, add coconut oil.

ELEPHANT YAM DRY ROAST

Ingredients

1.	Elephant Yam (peeled)	-	2 cups
2.	Shallots	-	12
3.	Garlic cloves	-	6
4.	Ginger	-	1 small piece
5.	Curry leaves	-	1 sprig
6.	Pepper powder	-	½ tsp
7.	Turmeric powder	-	½ tsp
8.	Garam masala powder	-	¼ tsp
9.	Oil	-	1 large spoon
10.	Water, Salt	-	as required

Slice the yam in thin cubical pieces lengthwise. Cook in salt and water till water evaporates. Finely chop ingredients 2 to 5. Sauté these in oil. Add salt. Once sautéed, add ingredients 6 to 8 and cook further. Now put in the cooked yam, mix and simmer till it's well coated with the spices.

ERISHERI

Ingredients

1.	Pumpkin (peeled and diced)	-	250 g
2.	Green chilies (finely chopped)	-	4
3.	Coconut (grated)	-	1 half
4.	Garlic cloves	-	2
5.	Cumin seeds	-	½ tsp
6.	Coconut oil	-	1 large spoon
7.	Mustard seeds	-	½ tsp
8.	Coconut grated	-	1 large spoon
9.	Shallots (finely chopped)	-	1
10.	Curry leaves	-	1 sprig
11.	Water	-	1 cup
12.	Salt	-	to taste

Cook ingredients 1 and 2 with salt and water well. Mash well. Grind ingredients 3, 4 and 5 well. Mix this into the mashed pumpkin mixture along with salt. Switch on the flame. When the mixture starts frothing, switch off the flame. Crackle mustard seeds in hot coconut oil and sauté finely chopped shallots, curry leaves and ingredient 8 nicely. Pour this into the mashed pumpkin mixture.

FAST TO COOK CURRY

Ingredients

1.	Shallots (thinly sliced)	-	1 cup
2.	Garlic cloves	-	5
3.	Ginger (finely chopped)	-	1 small piece
4.	Green chilies (finely chopped)	-	2
5.	Curry leaves	-	1 sprig
6.	Tomato (big, finely chopped)	-	1
7.	Oil	-	1 spoon
8.	Water	-	1 cup
9.	Salt	-	to taste
10.	Mustard seeds	-	as required
11.	Red chili powder	-	½ tsp
12.	Coriander powder	-	¼ tsp
13.	Turmeric powder	-	¼ tsp
14.	Garam masala powder	-	as required

Pop mustard seeds in oil. Add ingredients 1 to 6 and sauté well. Add in the ingredients 11 to 14 and sauté further. Once nicely sautéed, pour in water and let it boil. Simmer thereafter and cook till the gravy thickens.

GINGER CURRY

Ingredients

1.	Ginger (finely chopped)	-	1 large piece
2.	Green chilies (finely chopped)	-	5
3.	Shallots (finely chopped)	-	10
4.	Garlic Cloves (finely chopped)	-	4
5.	Curry leaves	-	2 sprigs
6.	Oil	-	1 large spoon
7.	Water, salt	-	as required
8.	Jaggery(grated)	-	2 tsp
9.	Coconut oil	-	1 large spoon
10.	Mustard seeds & onion (chopped)	-	a little
11.	Coconut (grated)	-	1 half
12.	Tamarind (small lemon sized)	-	one
13.	Red chili powder	-	1 tsp
14.	Turmeric Powder	-	1 tsp
15.	Coriander powder	-	½ tsp
16.	Fenugreek powder	-	a little

Soak tamarind in water and extract the pulp. Roast grated coconut well. Add the powders and roast further. Grind into a paste. Heat oil. Add ingredients 1 to 5 and sauté well. Put in the tamarind pulp, water and salt and let it come to a boil. Once it is cooked, add in the paste and mix well. Add grated jaggery. Lower the flame and let the gravy thicken. Pop mustard seeds in coconut oil and sauté chopped onion in it. Pour this oil into the ginger gravy. Boil again and switch off the flame.

KAALLAN

Ingredients

1.	Raw banana diced	-	2 cups
2.	Pepper powder	-	2 tsp
3.	Turmeric powder	-	1 tsp
4.	Curd	-	1½ cups
5.	Coconut (grated)	-	1 half
6.	Green chilies	-	5
7.	Dry red chilies	-	2
8.	Coconut oil	-	1 large spoon
9.	Fenugreek powder	-	½ tsp
10.	Salt	-	to taste
11.	Curry leaves	-	1 sprig
12.	Mustard seeds	-	a little

Cook banana with pepper powder, turmeric powder, salt and water. Grind ingredients 5 and 6 and add to the above cooked mixture. Simmer and add beaten curd into the mixture and boil. Crackle mustard seeds in coconut oil and sauté dry red chilies and curry leaves also. Pour this into the cooked banana mixture, add fenugreek powder & mix well. Remove from fire.

CHINESE POTATO DRY ROAST

Ingredients

1. Chinese potato   -   ½ kg
   (peeled, washed and thinly sliced)
2. Coconut slices   -   ½ cup
3. Shallots   -   30
4. Garlic Cloves   -   10
5. Ginger   -   1
   (medium sized)
6. Green chilies   -   3
7. Curry leaves   -   2 sprigs
8. Oil   -   2 large spoons
9. Water, salt   -   as required
10. Red chili powder   -   ½ tsp
11. Turmeric Powder   -   ½ tsp
12. Pepper powder   -   ¼ tsp

Finely chop shallots, garlic cloves, ginger & green chilies. Mix the Chinese potato, chopped ingredients, curry leaves, salt, water and cook. Once water reduces to half, add roasted spice powder into it and cook. Once the entire liquid evaporates, pour oil and mix thoroughly. Sauté well.

WHITE GOURD CURRY

Ingredients

1.	White gourd/ Ash gourd (chopped)	-	1 cup
2.	Green chilies (slit ¾th, lengthwise)	-	4
3.	Tomato medium sized (chopped)	-	1
4.	Coconut (grated)	-	1 half
5.	Garlic cloves	-	3
6.	Shallots	-	6
7.	Cumin	-	¼ tsp
8.	Turmeric powder	-	½ tsp
9.	Coconut oil	-	1 large spoon
10.	Mustard	-	a little
11.	Salt	-	to taste
12.	Curry leaves	-	1 sprig
13.	Water	-	2 cups

Cook ingredients 1 to 3 with salt and 1 cup water. Grind ingredients 4 to 7. Add this to the cooked vegetables. Add the remaining water, turmeric powder, curry leaves and cook. Garnish with mustard seeds popped in coconut oil.

SPICY PUMPKIN CURRY

Ingredients

1.	Pumpkin (Chopped)	-	2½ cups
2.	Tomato (chopped)	-	2
3.	Green chilies (slit ¾th; lengthwise)	-	4
4.	Onion (chopped)	-	1 big
5.	Garlic cloves	-	12 big
6.	Ginger	-	1 small piece
7.	Curry leaves	-	1 sprig
8.	Mustard seeds	-	a little
9.	Salt, water	-	as required
10.	Oil	-	2 large spoons
11.	Coconut oil	-	1 spoon
12.	Red chili powder	-	2 tsp
13.	Coriander powder	-	1 tsp
14.	Turmeric powder	-	1 tsp
15.	Garam masala powder	-	½ tsp

Sauté ingredients 1, 2 and 3 in oil. Grind ingredients 5 and 6 together. Grind the onion as well. Sauté the ground pastes in oil one after another. Add coconut oil, curry leaves, powders and sauté till the raw smell subsides. Add salt, water and sautéed pumpkin mixture. Simmer and blend well.

DRUMSTICK POTATO CURRY

Ingredients

1.	Drumsticks (thick and long)	-	3
2.	Potatoes	-	2
3.	Onion (chopped)	-	1
4.	Garlic cloves	-	10
5.	Ginger	-	1 small piece
6.	Tomato (chopped)	-	1
7.	Curry leaves	-	1 sprig
8.	Oil	-	2 large spoons
9.	Vinegar	-	1 spoon
10.	Salt, water	-	as required
11.	Red chili powder	-	2 tsp
12.	Coriander powder	-	1 tsp
13.	Turmeric powder	-	1 tsp
14.	Fennel Powder	-	1 tsp

Peel the drumsticks and cut it into strips. Slice potatoes into ½ inch pieces. Grind garlic and ginger into a paste. Grind onion into a paste. Heat oil in a wok and sauté ingredients 1, 2 and 6. Once sautéed, remove from the wok and keep aside. Now sauté the pastes. Once sautéed, add ingredients 11 to 14 and sauté well. Add water and salt into the wok. Put in the sautéed vegetables, vinegar and curry leaves into the wok. Mix well. Simmer and cook till the vegetables are properly coated with the gravy.

LEMON CURRY

Ingredients

1.	Curry lemon or Meyer lemon	-	½
2.	Green chilies (finely chopped)	-	2
3.	Garlic Cloves	-	5 (finely chopped)
4.	Shallots	-	6(finely (chopped)
5.	Ginger (finely chopped)	-	1 small piece
6.	Curry leaves	-	1 sprig (chopped)
7.	Oil	-	1 spoon
8.	Water	-	1 cup
9.	Tamarind	-	as needed
10.	Coconut oil	-	1 spoon
11.	Mustard seeds & Curry leaves	-	a little
12.	Onion (thinly chopped)	-	½ tsp
13.	Salt	-	to taste
14.	Red chili powder	-	1½ tsp
15.	Coriander powder	-	½ tsp
16.	Turmeric Powder	-	½ tsp
17.	Fenugreek powder	-	as required
18.	Coconut	-	½

Peel and deseed curry lemon, remove the pith and membrane. Dice lemon flakes finely. Grate coconut and dry roast till light brown. Now add all the powders and cook till the raw smell subsides. Wet grind this mixture.

Heat oil in a wok. Sauté ingredients 2 to 6. Then add lemon pieces and sauté till brown colour. Now add tamarind pulp, salt and cook. Once the liquid thickens, add coconut paste, water and bring to a boil. Simmer and let the gravy thicken. Pop in mustard seeds in coconut oil, add the chopped onion and curry leaves and sauté. Mix it in the lemon gravy well.

OLAN

Ingredients

1. White gourd/ Ash gourd   -   2 cups
   (chopped in1inch sized cubes)
2. Green chilies   -   4
3. Brown peas   -   ¼ cup
4. Coconut (grated)   -   1 half
5. Coconut oil   -   1 spoon
6. Salt   -   to taste

Cook brown peas in salt and water. Cook ash gourd, green chilies in salt and water. Add cooked brown peas into this mixture.
Extract coconut milk from the grated coconut. Add this coconut milk into the cooked mixture. Lastly add coconut oil into the mixture and mix.

STIR FRIED YARD LONG BEANS

Ingredients

1.	Yard long beans	-	250 g
2.	Green chilies	-	4 (sliced lengthwise)
3.	Onion (small)	-	1 (thinly sliced)
4.	Shallots	-	5 (thinly sliced)
5.	Garlic cloves	-	4 (chopped)
6.	Coconut slices	-	½ cup
7.	Curry leaves	-	1 sprig
8.	Turmeric powder	-	½ tsp
9.	Salt	-	to taste
10.	Oil	-	1 large spoon
11.	Water	-	¼ cup

Cut the beans in ½ inch sized strips. Heat oil in a wok. Add turmeric powder and ingredients 1 to 7. Sauté well. Once sautéed, add salt & water. Simmer and cook till the water dry up.

PULISHERI

Ingredients

1.	Curd	-	1½ cups
2.	Coconut (grated)	-	½ cup
3.	Dried red chilies	-	2 (break each into three)
4.	Cumin seeds	-	½ tsp
5.	Garlic cloves	-	2
6.	Shallots	-	1

(finely chopped)

7.	Curry leaves	-	1 sprig
8.	Mustard seeds	-	½ tsp
9.	Oil	-	1 large spoon
10.	Salt, water	-	as required
11.	Fenugreek powder	-	1 pinch
12.	Turmeric powder	-	¼ tsp

Beat curd into a smooth consistency. Add water, salt and blend well. Grind ingredients 2, 4 & 5 finely. Crackle mustard seeds in hot oil and sauté ingredient6 in it. Add curry leaves, dried red chilies, and ingredients 11 and 12. Sauté well. Now add beaten curd. Heat it well and remove from flame.

SAMBAR

Ingredients

1.	Lentil	-	1 small cup
2.	Onion (large)	-	1
3.	Shallots	-	10
4.	Garlic cloves	-	4
5.	Green chilies	-	4
6.	Yam (cubed)	-	1 cup
7.	White gourd (cubed)	-	1 cup
8.	Drumsticks (sliced)	-	2
9.	Raw Banana (cubed)	-	1
10.	Lady finger(cut and sautéed in oil)	-	4
11.	Yard long beans (slit lengthwise)	-	a few
12.	Tomato (large)	-	1 (chopped)
13.	Vinegar	-	1 large spoon
14.	Coconut oil	-	1 spoon
15.	Curry leaves, coriander leaves	-	½ cup
16.	Salt, water	-	as required
17.	Red chili powder	-	2 tsp
18.	Coriander powder	-	2 tsp
19.	Turmeric powder	-	1 tsp
20.	Asafetida powder	-	½ tsp
21.	Fenugreek powder	-	¼ tsp
22.	Cumin powder & mustard seed powder (combined)	-	½ tsp

Pressure cook lentil with salt and ingredients 2 to 5.Further add ingredients 6 to 12 into the cooker, salt, water and pressure cook. Do not overcook.

Heat oil. Pop mustard seeds, add the curry leaves and the powders except asafoetida and sauté. Now add asafoetida. Pour this mixture into the cooked veggies. Add vinegar, water (as required), salt and mix well. Let it come to a boil. Simmer till the required consistency is attained. Switch off the flame. Garnish with coriander leaves.

TOMATO GRAVY CURRY

Ingredients

1.	Tomato (big; finely chopped)	-	2
2.	Onion (small; finely chopped)	-	1
3.	Shallots (finely chopped)	-	15
4.	Garlic cloves (2 finely chopped, 2 for grinding)	-	4
5.	Ginger (finely chopped)	-	1 small piece
6.	Green chilies (finely chopped)	-	3
7.	Curry leaves	-	1 sprig
8.	Coconut (grated)	-	1 half
9.	Water	-	2½ cups
10.	Coconut Oil	-	1 spoon
11.	Salt	-	to taste
12.	Mustard seeds	-	as required
13.	Fennel seeds	-	as required
14.	Turmeric powder	-	½ tsp
15.	Vinegar	-	1 tsp

Heat oil in a wok. Sauté ingredients 1 to 6 very well. Add curry leaves and sauté well. Once done, add 1 cup water, salt and cover with a lid. Let it simmer. Blend well. Wet grind grated coconut, 2 garlic cloves & fennel seeds. Add this ground mixture and remaining water to the sautéed mixture. Simmer and thicken the gravy. Switch off the flame once the curry froths. Pop mustard seeds in coconut oil and add into the curry. Put on low flame till it boils. Mix well.

SHALLOT CURRY

Ingredients

1. Shallots   -   250 gm
   (thinly sliced)
2. Green chilies   -   3
   (slit into two and cut into three)
3. Garlic Cloves   -   6(chopped)
4. Curry leaves   -   2 sprigs
5. Tomato   -   2 (chopped)
6. Coconut slices   -   1 large spoon
7. Vinegar   -   1 dessert spoon
8. Salt, water   -   as per requirement
9. Oil   -   1 dessert spoon
10. Coconut oil   -   1 dessert spoon

For the paste

11. Coconut (grated)   -   ½
12. Red chili powder   -   2 tsp
13. Coriander powder   -   1 tsp
14. Turmeric Powder   -   1 tsp
15. Fenugreek powder   -   a little

Sauté ingredients 1 to 6 in oil well. Add water, vinegar, salt and cook. Roast grated coconut to a golden colour. Add ingredients 12 to 15 and sauté further. Grind to a paste. Add this paste to the sautéed onion mixture. Simmer once it starts boiling. Cook till the gravy thickens. Pop mustard seeds in coconut oil and pour into the onion curry.

POTATO YARD LONG BEANS MASALA CURRY

Ingredients

1.	Yard long beans	-	1 cup(cut in 1" size)
2.	Potato	-	2 (cut in thin cuboids)
3.	Onion	-	1 (thinly sliced)
4.	Shallots	-	5 (thinly sliced)
5.	Garlic Cloves	-	6 (finely chopped)
6.	Ginger (finely chopped)	-	1 small piece
7.	Green chilies	-	2 (slit into 4)
8.	Tomato (chopped)	-	1
9.	Curry leaves	-	1 sprig
10.	Salt	-	to taste
11.	Oil	-	1 big spoon
12.	Water	-	1 cup
13.	Red chili powder	-	1 tsp
14.	Coriander powder	-	½ tsp
15.	Turmeric powder	-	½ tsp
16.	Pepper powder	-	¼ tsp
17.	Garam masala powder	-	¼ tsp

Heat oil in a wok. Sauté ingredients 1 to 9 well. Once sautéed, add ingredients 13 to 17 and cook well. Add water and bring to a boil. Simmer and cook till the vegetables are well coated with the gravy.

STIR FRIED RAW BANANA

Ingredients

1. Raw banana   -   2
   (thinly striped into cuboids)
2. Green chilies   -   2
   (slit lengthwise and cut into four)
3. Shallots   -   5 (thinly sliced)
4. Garlic pods   -   2 (chopped)
5. Curry leaves   -   a little
6. Coconut Oil   -   1 spoon
7. Salt, Water   -   as required

Wash bananas well. Sauté ingredients 1 to 5 nicely in oil. Add salt and water. Mix well. Cook till water evaporates.

RAW BANANA UPPU CURRY

Ingredients

1.	Banana (large; chopped)	-	3
2.	Coconut (grated)	-	1 half
3.	Green chilies	-	4
4.	Shallots	-	10
5.	Garlic cloves	-	3
6.	Cumin	-	¼ tsp
7.	Coconut oil	-	1 large spoon
8.	Curry leaves	-	1 sprig
9.	Mustard seeds	-	a little
10.	Salt, water	-	as required

Cook banana in salt and water. Grind ingredients 5 & 6. Coarse grind ingredients 3 and 4. Add coconut into it and coarse grind. Pound curry leaves. Add ground mixture and curry leaves to cooked banana. Boil, simmer and blend well. Crackle mustard seeds in coconut oil and pour. Mix well.

OKRA SAUTÉED WITH COCONUT

Ingredients

1. Lady finger/ Okra - 25
2. Grated coconut - 2 cups
3. Shallots - 15
   (Thinly sliced lengthwise)
4. Ginger - 1 small piece
   (finely chopped)
5. Garlic pods - 5
   (finely chopped)
6. Green chilies - 3
   (finely chopped)
7. Curry leaves - 1 sprig
8. Oil - 3 tsp
9. Salt - to taste
10. Mustard seeds - as required

Cut lady finger into four or five pieces. Finely slice each piece lengthwise. Pop mustard seeds in oil and sauté ingredients 3 to 7. Add salt and lady finger. Sauté further. Now add grated coconut and cook till done.

CHICKEN CURRY

Ingredients

1. Chicken pieces - 1 kg
2. Potato medium sized - 2
3. Cooking oil - 3 large spoons
4. Coconut oil - 2 large spoons
5. Vinegar - 2 tsp
6. Onion (thinly sliced) - 2
7. Shallots (thinly sliced) - 20
8. Garlic cloves (thinly sliced) - 10
9. Ginger (thinly sliced) - 1 tsp
10. Green chilies - 3 (Each cut into four)
11. Curry leaves - 1 sprig
12. Tomato (thinly diced) - 1 large
13. Coconut(grated) - 1 big piece
14. Water - 2 cups
15. Salt - to taste
16. Curd - 1 tbsp
17. Pepper powder - 2 tsp
18. Coriander powder - 1 tsp
19. Fennel powder - ½ tsp
20. Turmeric powder - ½ tsp
21. Garam masala powder - ½ tsp

Soak ingredients 17 to 21 in water or grind them into a paste. Clean chicken pieces and marinate in curd for ½ an hour. Peel and thinly slice potatoes. Sauté the potato roundels in oil. Sprinkle a little salt. Keep aside. Sauté the onions, shallot, ginger, garlic and green chilies in the wok. Add tomatoes and curry leaves. Add salt and the soaked masala into the mixture. Add the chicken pieces.

Grind coconut and strain the first extract (thick coconut milk). Add water and strain the 2nd and 3rd extracts (thin coconut milk). Add the 2nd and 3rd extracts and sautéed potatoes into the chicken mixture. Cook in low flame till it boils and the chicken is done. Pop mustard seeds in the hot coconut oil and pour into the chicken mixture. Add vinegar and lastly the first extract of coconut milk. Mix well.

CHICKEN ROAST

Ingredients

1. Chicken   -   1 kg
2. Curd   -   ¼ cup
3. Cooking oil   -   ½ cup
4. Coconut oil   -   2 large spoons
5. Onion (Big)   -   3
6. Shallots   -   1 cup
7. Garlic cloves   -   ½ cup
8. Ginger thinly sliced   -   ½ cup
9. Green chilies (slit)   -   4
10. Curry leaves   -   2 sprigs
11. Tomato   -   3
12. Salt   -   to taste
13. Red chili powder   -   1 dessert spoon
14. Pepper powder   -   ½ tsp
15. Turmeric powder   -   1 tsp
16. Coriander powder   -   2 tsp
17. Garam masala powder   -   ½ tsp

Clean the chicken, drain water and marinate in curd. Sauté onion, shallots, garlic, ginger and green chilies in a wok. Once sautéed, add salt, tomatoes and curry leaves. Add ingredients 13 to 17 to the mixture and fry well. Drop the chicken pieces once the masala is done. Cover and cook till the chicken become tender. Evaporate water so that the chicken pieces are well coated with the gravy. Add coconut oil and fry chicken further.

CHICKEN PICKLE

Ingredients

1.	Chicken (boneless; cut into small pieces)	-	1 kg
2.	Garlic cloves (halved lengthwise)	-	45
3.	Ginger juliennes	-	1 big piece
4.	Green chillies	-	4
5.	Curry leaves	-	1 sprig
6.	Salt boiled in ½ glass water	-	1 tsp
7.	Oil	-	1 cup
8.	Vinegar	-	2 tsp
9.	Coconut oil	-	2 tsp

To be ground to a paste

10.	Red Chili powder	-	1 large spoon
11.	Pepper powder	-	½ tsp
12.	Turmeric powder	-	1 tsp
13.	Shallots	-	12
14.	Garlic cloves	-	2
15.	Ginger	-	1 small piece

Marinade for chicken

16.	Pepper powder	-	½ tsp
17.	Turmeric powder	-	½ tsp
18.	Garam Masala powder	-	a little
19.	Salt	-	to taste

Marinate chicken with ingredients 16 to 19 and refrigerate for 1 hr. Heat oil in a wok and fry chicken pieces. Keep aside. Sauté ingredients 2 to 5 in oil (strain the oil). Keep aside. Add coconut oil into the remaining oil and sauté the paste. Add water boiled with salt and mix. Put in the chicken pieces and sautéed ingredients 2 to 5 and let the mixture boil. Remove from flame. Cool and store.

EGG ROAST

Ingredients

1.	Eggs (boiled & deshelled)	-	4
2.	Onion (medium) (thinly sliced lengthwise)	-	1
3.	Shallots	-	10 (Thinly sliced)
4.	Garlic cloves (finely chopped)	-	4
5.	Ginger (finely chopped)	-	1 small piece
6.	Green chilies (slit lengthwise and cut into two)	-	2
7.	Curry leaves	-	1 sprig
8.	Coconut oil	-	1½ large spoons
9.	Mustard seeds	-	¼ tsp
10.	Tomato (large) (finely chopped)	-	1
11.	Salt, water	-	as required
12.	Red chili powder	-	½ tsp
13.	Turmeric powder	-	¼ tsp
14.	Pepper powder	-	¼ tsp
15.	Garam Masala powder	-	¼ tsp

Heat oil in a wok. Crackle mustard seeds and sauté ingredients 2, 3, 4, 5 and 6 well. Add salt, ingredients 12, 13, 14, 15 and sauté well. Add curry leaves and sauté further. Sprinkle a little water and cook. Put in the eggs and cook till the eggs are well coated with the mixture.

EGG POTATO CURRY

Ingredients

1.	Eggs (boiled & deshelled)	-	4
2.	Potato (medium sized) (each peeled and cut into 8 pieces)	-	2
3.	Onion (medium sized; thinly sliced)	-	1
4.	Shallots (thinly sliced)	-	6
5.	Garlic cloves (finely chopped)	-	2
6.	Green chilies (slit lengthwise & cut into two)	-	2
7.	Ginger (finely chopped)	-	1 small piece
8.	Curry leaves	-	1 sprig
9.	Tomato (large sized) (finely chopped)	-	1
10.	Water	-	½ glass
11.	Coconut oil	-	1 large spoon
12.	Oil	-	3 tsp
13.	Mustard seeds	-	¼ tsp
14.	Salt	-	to taste
15.	Red chili powder	-	½ tsp
16.	Coriander powder	-	½ tsp
17.	Turmeric powder	-	¼ tsp
18.	Pepper powder	-	¼ tsp
19.	Garam Masala powder	-	¼ tsp

Slice each egg into four pieces. Heat oil in a wok and sauté potato pieces. Once sautéed, keep separately. Now add coconut oil and sauté ingredients 3 to 8 well. Add salt and ingredients 15 to 19 till the raw aroma subsides. Now put in the sautéed potatoes, water and cook till the potatoes are done. Lastly add in the egg pieces. Simmer for 10 minutes.

PRAWN DRY ROAST

Ingredients

1.	Prawn (deshelled & deveined)	-	½ kg
2.	Shallot (sliced)	-	45
3.	Garlic cloves (finely chopped)	-	10
4.	Ginger (finely chopped)	-	1 medium piece
5.	Green chilies (finely chopped)	-	2
6.	Curry leaves	-	1 sprig
7.	Coconut (thinly sliced)	-	¼ cup
8.	Fish tamarind (soaked in water) (sliced)	-	6
9.	Water	-	½ cup
10.	Salt	-	to taste
11.	Cooking oil	-	2 large spoons
12.	Coconut oil	-	2 large spoons
13.	Red chili powder	-	½ tsp
14.	Coriander powder	-	½ tsp
15.	Pepper powder	-	½ tsp
16.	Turmeric powder	-	½ tsp
17.	Garam masala powder	-	¼ tsp

Cut prawns into 2 pieces each. Heat oil in a wok and sauté ingredients 2 to 5. Add sliced coconut and sauté. Then add salt and curry leaves. Once sautéed, add ingredients 13 to 17 and fry well. Add prawns and sauté. Add water and let the mixture come to a boil. Add salt and fish tamarind. Simmer till the entire liquid evaporates. Add coconut oil and cook till the prawns are well coated with the gravy.

FISH CURRY

Ingredients

1.	Fish	-	½ kg
2.	Red chili powder	-	2 tsp
3.	Coriander powder	-	1 tsp
4.	Turmeric powder	-	½ tsp
5.	Fenugreek Powder	-	1 pinch
6.	Shallots	-	15
7.	Garlic cloves	-	2
8.	Ginger (Medium sized piece)	-	1(keep half separately)
9.	Curry leaves	-	1 sprig
10.	Salt	-	to taste
11.	Fish tamarind (slit)	-	4 (soaked in water)
12.	Oil	-	2 tbsp
13.	Coconut oil	-	1 large spoon
14.	Water	-	1½ cup
15.	Mustard seeds	-	as per requirement.

Wet grind ingredients 2 to 8. Heat oil in a wok and sauté this paste. Once sautéed, add water and soaked fish tamarind. Add salt, fish, curry leaves, ginger juliennes (from the half kept separately). Bring to a boil. Simmer till the gravy thickens. Pop mustard seeds in coconut oil and pour to this mixture. Remove from the flame once it boils again.

FISH PAPPAS

Ingredients

1. Rohu pieces - ½ kg
   [Pearl spot is the best option for pappas.]
2. Green chilies (half slit) - 6
3. Garlic cloves (slit lengthwise) - 7
4. Ginger - 1
   (medium sized; thinly sliced)
5. Shallots - 6
   (medium sized; thinly sliced)
6. Curry leaves - 1 sprig
7. Mustard seeds - ¼ tsp
8. Shallot (finely chopped) - 1
9. Coconut (grated and ground) - 1 half
10. Water - as required
11. Cooking oil - ½ cup
12. Coconut oil - 2 tsp
13. Fish Tamarind - 2
    (thin strips) (soaked in water)
14. Strain and extract the thick coconut milk. Add water and strain the second and third extracts.
15. a. Red chili powder - 1 tsp
    b. Coriander powder - 1 tsp
    c. Turmeric powder - ½ tsp
    d. Garam Masala powder - ¼ tsp

Coat the fish pieces with turmeric powder and salt. Heat oil in a wok and fry the fish. Sauté ingredients 2 to 5. Keep separately. Now sauté the powders well, pour in the second and third extracts, add the sautéed ingredients, fish tamarind and let it come to a boil. Now add in the fish pieces and curry leaves. Simmer until the liquid evaporates. Pop mustard seeds in coconut oil, add the chopped onion and sauté. Pour into the fish mixture. Once the gravy thickens, add the first extract, mix well and switch off the flame. (Do not let the curry boil).

FISH PEERA PATTICHATHU

Ingredients
(Mackerel/Sardine/Tuna/ Convict surgeonfish / white sardine can be used.}

1.	Fish	-	½ kg
2.	Coconut grated	-	1 half
3.	Green chillies	-	4
4.	Dried red chillies	-	4
5.	Shallots	-	18
6.	Garlic cloves	-	3
7.	Ginger	-	1 piece
8.	Curry leaves	-	1 sprig
9.	Fish Tamarind (slit)	-	5 (Soaked in water)
10.	Coconut oil	-	1 large spoon
11.	Turmeric powder	-	¼ tsp
12.	Water	-	1 cup
13.	Salt	-	to taste

Cut fish into small pieces. Pound both chilies in a mortar. Add shallots into the mixture and pound. Add garlic and ginger and pound further. Mix the pounded mixture with grated coconut, curry leaves, turmeric powder, salt, water, fish and fish tamarind. Mix well and cook at high flame till it boils. Then simmer till the liquid reduces to half. Add coconut oil and mix carefully. Switch off the flame once the entire liquid evaporates.

FISH POLLICHHATHU

Ingredients

1.	Pearl spot or Mackerel	-	½ kg
2.	Black pepper powder	-	5 tsp
3.	Turmeric powder	-	1 tsp
4.	Fennel powder	-	½ tsp
5.	Shallots	-	8
6.	Garlic cloves	-	5
7.	Ginger	-	1 piece
8.	Salt	-	to taste
9.	Coconut oil	-	as required
10.	Water	-	½ cup
11.	Banana leaf	-	2 pieces

Clean and closely slit the fish. Grind ingredients 2 to 8 and apply on the fish. Apply coconut oil on the banana leaf and lay the leaf as the base in a wok. Now place the fish side by side on the leaf. Pour a little coconut oil all over the fish. Pour water below the banana leaf to prevent it from getting burnt. Cover the fish with another banana leaf and place the wok on flame. Place a lid on the wok. Lower the flame once the mixture heats up well. When the fish is done on one side, flip the fish carefully. Water under the leaf should be replenished. Cook fish till it is fully wrapped in the gravy.

FISH THODUCURRY

Ingredients

1.	Fish chunks (of one's choice)	-	½ kg
2.	Shallots	-	10
3.	Garlic Cloves	-	2
4.	Ginger	-	1 small piece
5.	Curry leaves	-	1 sprig
6.	Fish tamarind (thinly sliced)	-	4 pieces
7.	Coconut oil	-	2½ large spoons
8.	Mustard seeds	-	¼ tsp
9.	Water	-	little
10.	Salt	-	to taste
	To be ground		
11.	Red chili powder	-	2 tsp
12.	Turmeric powder	-	¼ tsp
13.	Fenugreek powder	-	1 pinch

Clean the fish chunks well. Grind ingredients 2,3 and 4 along with the three powders to a fine paste. Soak the cleaned and washed fish tamarind in water. Heat a little coconut oil in a wok and add mustard seeds and curry leaves. Let them splutter. Keep aside. Heat the remaining oil and sauté the ground paste till the raw smell subsides. Add water, salt and soaked tamarind into this paste and bring to a boil. Now add the fish pieces gently. Cover and cook on low heat and bring it to the required consistency. Now add sautéed mustard seeds and curry leaves into it. Mix well.

FISH VATTI PATTICHATHU

Ingredients

1. Fish pieces   -   ½ kg
   (Fish like Pearl spot, Tilapia, Mullet can be used)
2. Oil   -   1 tbsp
3. Coconut oil   -   2 tbsp
4. Onion (thinly sliced)   -   2
5. Shallots(thinly sliced)   -   25
6. Green chilies   -   4
   (slit and cut into two)
7. Dried red chilies   -   5
   (Broken into three pieces each)
8. Ginger medium sized   -   1 piece
   (finely chopped)
9. Curry leaves   -   1 sprig
10. Garlic cloves   -   4
    (finely chopped)
11. Turmeric powder   -   ¼ tsp
12. Salt   -   to taste
13. Water   -   1 cup
14. Fish Tamarind (slit)   -   5 (Soaked in water)

Heat oil in a wok. Sauté ingredients 4 to 10. Add salt and sauté further. Once sautéed, add water, fish tamarind, salt and fish. Mix well. Let it boil. Further simmer till the fish is coated with the gravy well. Turn the fish carefully. The mixture should be evenly poured over the fish so that the gravy is uniformly absorbed.

SEER FISH SAUTEED WITH COCONUT

Ingredients

1.	Seer fish pieces	-	250 gm
2.	Coconut (grated)	-	1 half
3.	Shallots	-	12
4.	Garlic pods	-	3
5.	Ginger	-	1 small piece
6.	Green chilies	-	6
7.	Curry leaves	-	1 sprig
8.	Fish tamarind (slit)	-	4 pieces
9.	Coconut oil	-	1 large spoon
10.	Water	-	½ cup
11.	Turmeric powder	-	½ tsp
12.	Mustard seeds	-	as required

Mix fish, fish tamarind, salt, water and cook. Once water evaporates, put off the flame. Separate fish pieces and mash it after removing the bones. Pound ingredients 3 to 6.Heat coconut oil in a wok. Pop mustard seeds and sauté the pounded ingredients. Add grated coconut, curry leaves, turmeric powder, salt, fish and cook well.

FISH PICKLE

Ingredients

1. Boneless fish (e.g. Tuna)   -   ½ kg
   (cut into small pieces)
2. Garlic cloves slit   -   20
3. Ginger (juliennes)   -   1-inch
4. Green chilies; half slit   -   4
5. Curry leaves   -   1 sprig
6. Salt   -   1 tsp
   (boiled in ½ glass water)
7. Oil   -   1 cup
8. Vinegar   -   2 large spoons
9. Coconut oil   -   2 tsp
10. To be ground to a paste
11. Red chili powder   -   1 tbsp
12. Turmeric powder   -   1 tsp
13. Fenugreek powder   -   1 pinch
14. Shallots   -   10
15. Garlic cloves   -   2
16. Ginger   -   1 small piece

For the marinade
17. Red chili powder   -   ½ tsp
18. Turmeric powder   -   ½ tsp
19. Salt   -   as per requirement

Coat the fish with the marinade and refrigerate for about 1 hr. Heat oil in a wok and fry fish pieces till crisp. In a little oil, fry ingredients 2 to 5 and keep aside. Garlic should not get over fried. Add coconut oil to the remnant oil in the wok and sauté the paste. Care should be taken so that the paste doesn't burn. Add boiled water containing salt into the mixture. Mix well and add fried fish pieces; fried ingredients 2 to 5 and vinegar. Bring to a boil and keep aside. Store in an air tight container after it cools down.

BIRYANI

Ingredients

1.	Mutton/Chicken	-	1 kg
2.	Oil	-	½ cup
3.	a. Onion (finely diced)	-	2 cups
	b. Turmeric powder	-	1 tsp
4.	a. Garlic paste	-	4 tsp
	b. Ginger paste	-	2 tsp
5.	a. Coriander	-	2 tsp
	b. Red Chili powder	-	1½ tsp
6.	a. Curd	-	½ cup
	b. Lemon juice	-	1 large spoon
	c. Raisin paste	-	4 tsp
	d. Cashew nut paste	-	2 tbsp
	e. Salt	-	to taste
7.	a. Coriander leaves	-	½ cup
	b. Mint leaves	-	a little
8.	Biryani rice	-	2 glass
9.	Oil	-	½ cup
10.	Onion (thinly sliced)	-	½ cup
11.	a. Cinnamon	-	4
	b. Cloves	-	12
	c. Green cardamom	-	4
12.	Boiled water	-	5 glass

Heat oil in a wok. Sauté finely diced onion to golden brown. Add turmeric powder, garlic paste and ginger paste into the sautéed onion and cook till the raw smell diminishes. Add coriander powder and red chili powder into the mixture and sauté till properly done. Add meat and ingredient no. 6 into the wok. Add the required amount of water and cook till the meat is tender and the gravy thickens. Mix coriander leaves and sautéed mint leaves into the gravy.

For Rice: - Soak rice in water. Drain and keep aside. Fry thinly sliced onion till they are brown and crispy. Remove from wok and store in an air tight container. Fry ingredient no. 11 in hot oil followed by soaked rice. Stir till the rice is crisp. Add salt and boiled water into rice. Stir and let it boil. Simmer with the lid closed. When the rice is done, pour ghee and mix. Now layer rice on a flat oiled plate. Sprinkle saffron color dissolved in milk and fried onions over rice. Spread cooked meat over this layer. Repeat the process. Mix the layers well and transfer to a thick bottomed pot. Cover it with a lid. Place this pot on a hot tawa and place another preheated tawa on the lid. Cook for about 12 to 15 mins. on a medium heat. Once done switch off and allow to rest.

CUTLET

Ingredients

1.	Mutton(minced)	-	½ kg
2.	Onions	-	2
3.	Shallots	-	15
4.	Ginger	-	1 big piece
5.	Garlic cloves	-	1 tbsp
6.	Green chilies	-	3
7.	Curry leaves	-	1 sprig
8.	Salt	-	to taste
9.	Potatoes	-	2
10.	Red chili powder	-	1 tsp
11.	Turmeric powder	-	½ tsp
12.	Coriander powder	-	½ tsp
13.	Garam masala powder	-	¼tsp
14.	Vinegar	-	1 large spoon
15.	Egg	-	1
16.	Bread crumbs	-	½ cup
17.	Oil for frying	-	½ liter
18.	Water	-	½ cup

Wash mutton, drain water and keep aside. Chop ingredients2 to 6 into tiny pieces. Add these ingredients with mutton along with chopped curry leaves, salt, vinegar and water. Cook till the mutton is tender. Heat on flame till the entire liquid evaporates. Beat egg and keep aside. Heat oil in a wok. Sauté ingredients 10 to 12. Add mashed potatoes, garam masala powder into the mixture and mix thoroughly. Shape them into cutlets. Dip each cutlet in egg wash and roll on bread crumbs. Heat oil as required and fry cutlets from both sides.

MASHED TAPIOCA WITH MUTTON

Ingredients

1. Tapioca   -   1½ kg
   (peeled and cut into medium sized chunks)
2. Mutton   -   1 kg
   (with bone & cut into pieces)
3. a. Shallots (sliced) - 25
   b. Garlic cloves (chopped) - 20
   c. Ginger (chopped) - 1 big piece
   d. Coconut (pieced/ cut into strips) - 1 half
   e. Curry leaves - as required
   f. Red chili powder - 1½ tsp
   g. Coriander powder - 1½ tsp
   h. Turmeric powder - 1 small spoon
   i. Garam masala powder - ½ large spoon
   j. Pepper powder - 1 large spoon
4. a. Coconut (grated) - 1 half
   b. Shallots - 5
   c. Green chilies - 3
   d. Curry leaves - 2 sprigs
5. Coconut oil - a little

Pressure cook mutton with ingredient 3. Boil tapioca in saltwater and drain water once done. Pound ingredient 4 coarsely and mix with boiled tapioca. Now add pressure cooked mutton with tapioca and warm. Add hot coconut oil into the mixture and mix well.

PEPPER LIVER

Ingredients

1. Goat liver   -   250 g
   (cut into small pieces)
2. Onion (small, finely chopped)   -   1
3. Shallots (finely chopped)   -   15
4. Garlic cloves   -   5
   (finely chopped)
5. Green chilies   -   2
   (finely chopped)
6. Ginger (finely chopped)   -   1 small piece
7. Curry leaves   -   1 sprig
8. Cooking oil   -   2 spoons
9. Coconut oil   -   1 spoon
10. Salt   -   ½ tsp
11. Pepper powder   -   ½ tsp
12. Turmeric powder   -   ½ tsp
13. Garam masala powder   -   ¼ tsp
14. Water   -   ½ cup

Sauté ingredients 2 to 6 in hot oil. Once sautéed, add ingredients 11 to 13, curry leaves and sauté further. Add salt and coconut oil. Put in liver pieces and add water. Mix properly and let it come to a boil. Simmer and cook. Switch off the flame once the liver is thoroughly coated with the mixture.

MUTTON CURRY

Ingredients

1. Mutton — 1 kg
   (cut in medium sized pieces)
2. Cooking oil — ½ cup
3. Coconut oil — 1 large spoon
4. Vinegar — 2 dessert spoons
5. Onion medium sized — 4
   (thinly sliced)
6. Shallots or pearl onions — ½ cup
7. Ginger — ½ cup
8. Garlic cloves — ½ cup
9. Green chilies(slit) — 6
10. Curry leaves — 2 sprigs
11. Tomato (thinly diced) — 2
12. Salt — to taste
13. Water — ½ cup
14. Pepper powder — 3 tsp
15. Garam masala powder — 1 tsp
16. Turmeric powder — 1 tsp
17. Coriander Powder — 2 tsp

Soak ingredients 14 to 17 in water. Clean mutton well. Drain water. Add vinegar, salt and water to mutton and pressure cook till the mutton is tender. Thinly slice onions and shallots. Finely dice garlic and ginger.

Heat oil in a wok. Sauté ingredients 5 to 9. Add curry leaves and tomato and sauté further till golden. Add the soaked ingredients 14 to 17. Fry well. Add cooked mutton and mix well. Simmer the flame once the mixture boils. Cover with a lid and cook till the mutton pieces are well coated with the gravy. It can be eaten with rice, Chapati, Palappam or Idiyappam.

MUTTON CHADACHHATH

Ingredients

1.	Mutton(Boneless)	-	½ kg
2.	Onion	-	1
3.	Shallots	-	½ cup
4.	Garlic cloves	-	1 tbsp
5.	Ginger	-	1 piece
6.	Green chilies (half slit)	-	5
7.	Tomato diced	-	2
8.	Curry leaves	-	1 sprig
9.	Pepper powder	-	1 tsp
10.	Turmeric powder	-	½ tsp
11.	Coriander powder	-	½ tsp
12.	Garam masala powder	-	¼ tsp
13.	Curd	-	2 tbsp
14.	Cooking oil	-	2 tbsp
15.	Coconut oil	-	1 tbsp
16.	Water	-	1 glass

Clean the mutton and freeze. Once frozen, pound it well in a mortar. Care to be taken that the mutton fibres do not separate out. Now grind the onion, garlic and ginger separately. Keep aside. Sauté mutton well in oil heated in a wok. Once done, keep separately. Sauté the ground onion in the oil followed by garlic and ginger. Once done, add shallots, green chilies, diced tomatoes, curry leaves and coconut oil. Fry well. Add ingredients 9 to 12 and fry well. Now add the mutton, curd and water. Mix well. Let it boil. Simmer it till the mutton gets cooked and is well coated with the gravy.

MUTTON DRY ROAST

Ingredients

1.	Mutton (cut into small pieces)	-	1 kg
2.	Cooking oil	-	½ cup
3.	Coconut oil	-	2 dessert spoons
4.	Vinegar	-	2 dessert spoons
5.	Onion (thinly sliced)	-	4
6.	Shallots	-	1 cup
7.	Garlic cloves	-	½ cup
8.	Ginger	-	½ cup
9.	Green chilies (thinly diced)	-	2
10.	Curry leaves	-	2 sprigs
11.	Tomato (thinly diced)	-	2
12.	Water	-	½ cup
13.	Salt	-	to taste
14.	Red chili powder	-	2 tsp
15.	Coriander powder	-	1 tsp
16.	Turmeric powder	-	1 tsp
17.	Pepper powder	-	½ tsp
18.	Garam masala powder	-	1 tsp

Heat oil in a wok. Sauté thinly sliced onions, thinly diced shallots, garlic cloves, ginger, green chilies well. Add tomatoes, curry leaves and salt. Sauté till golden color. Add ingredients 14 to 18 and fry. Add mutton and mix thoroughly. Add vinegar, salt, water to the above mixture and pressure cook till the mutton is tender. Heat 2 dessert spoons of coconut oil in a wok and transfer the contents of the pressure cooker to the wok. Mix and evaporate water till the gravy coats the mutton pieces.

COCONUT CHUTNEY

Ingredients

1.	Coconut (grated)	-	1 big half
2.	Red chili powder	-	2 tsp
3.	Shallots (medium)	-	1
4.	Curry leaves	-	2 sprigs
5.	Ginger (medium sized)	-	1 piece
6.	Coconut oil	-	1 large spoon
7.	Mustard seeds	-	a little
8.	Salt	-	to taste
9.	Vinegar	-	1 large spoon

Grind shallots and ginger well. Now add coconut, red chili powder and coarse grind. Coconut should not get finely ground. Crackle mustard seeds and sauté curry leaves in coconut oil and add the ground mixture. Sauté well. Add vinegar, salt and mix well.

MANGO CHUTNEY

Ingredients

1. Raw mango   -   1 large
   (peeled and diced)
2. Coconut (grated)   -   1 half
3. Green chilies   -   6
4. Shallots   -   30
5. Ginger   -   1 small piece
6. Salt   -   to taste
7. Curry leaves   -   2 sprigs

Grind mango with salt. Add shallots, green chilies, ginger and grind further. Coarse grind coconut and curry leaves. Add salt. Mix ground mango and coconut mixture with salt well.

FAST TO COOK CHUTNEY

Ingredients

1. Raw mango   -   ½ cup
   (peeled and diced)
2. Dried red chilies   -   7
3. Shallots   -   20
4. Coconut oil   -   1 tsp

Boil salt in a little water. Cool and soak mango flesh in it. Refrigerate for a week. Pound the dried chilies and shallots in a mortar using mortar. Keep aside and now pound raw mango flesh soaked in salt very well. (Drain salt water first). Mix the pounded dried chilies and shallots into mango well. Add coconut oil and mix once again.

GREEN CHILI PICKLE

Ingredients

1.	Capsicum and large sized green chilies	-	½ kg
2.	Vinegar	-	2 cups
3.	Salt	-	4 tsp
4.	Tamarind (lemon sized)	-	2 large pieces
5.	Sugar	-	3 tsp
6.	Oil	-	1 cup
7.	Ginger paste	-	8 tbsp
8.	Garlic paste	-	8 tbsp
9.	Fenugreek powder	-	1 tsp
10.	Cumin powder	-	1 tsp
11.	Asafetida powder	-	2 tsp

Cut green chilies and capsicum into 1-inch pieces. Strain and keep aside. Soak tamarind in vinegar and extract the pulp. Heat oil in a wok. Sauté chilies thoroughly. Keep separately. Now sauté the pastes well in oil. Thereafter put in the powders and sauté well. Add the tamarind pulp, salt, sugar, mix well and sauté. Now add chilies and mix well.

RAW MANGO MUSTARD PICKLE

Ingredients

1.	Raw mango	-	1 kg
2.	Red chili powder	-	2 large spoons
3.	Fenugreek powder	-	¼ tsp
4.	Mustard powder	-	¼ tsp
5.	Asafetida powder	-	½ tsp
6.	Water	-	1 cup
7.	Salt	-	4 tsp
8.	Oil	-	1 spoon
9.	Shallots (thinly chopped)	-	8
10.	Garlic cloves (thinly chopped)	-	6
11.	Ginger (finely chopped)	-	1 piece
12.	Green chilies (big) (finely chopped)	-	4
13.	Curry leaves	-	2 sprigs (chopped)
14.	Coconut oil	-	1 spoon
15.	Mustard seeds	-	½ tsp

Chop or dice mango into very small cubes/cuboids. Boil salt in water and keep aside. Heat oil and pop mustard seeds. Sauté ingredients 9 to 13. Once sautéed, add ingredients 2 to 5 and sauté. Add in the mango pieces and salt water. Mix well and switch off the flame. Store in a clean dry container once it cools.

LEMON PICKLE

Ingredients

1. Lemons - 4
   (cut into small pieces)
2. Green chilies
   (finely chopped) - 1
3. Ginger - 1 small piece
   (finely chopped)
4. Garlic cloves - 7 (small)
   (finely chopped)
5. Curry leaves - 1 sprig
6. Water - ¼ cup
7. Mustard seeds - ¼ tsp
8. Shallot - 1
   (finely chopped)
9. Salt - to taste
10. Cooking oil - 1 spoon
11. Coconut oil - 1 tsp
12. Vinegar - 1 tsp
13. Red chili powder - 1 tsp
14. Fenugreek powder - ¼ tsp
15. Asafetida powder - ¼ tsp

Crackle mustard seeds in coconut oil and sauté chopped shallot. Keep separately. Boil salt in water. Heat cooking oil and sauté ingredients 2 to 5.Once sautéed, separate them out of the wok. Sauté lemon pieces and then add ingredients 13 to 15. Add boiled salt water, vinegar, mustard seeds and shallots along with coconut oil. The lemon pieces should be well coated with the mixture.

GOOSEBERRY PICKLE

Ingredients

1. Gooseberry   -   ½ kg
2. Oil   -   1 large spoon
3. Green chilies (big)   -   4
    (Halved)
4. Garlic Cloves   -   20
    (Halved lengthwise)
5. Ginger   -   1 large piece
    (sliced similar to garlic)
6. Curry leaves   -   1 sprig
7. Salt   -   2 tsp
8. Water   -   as required
9. Mustard seeds   -   a little
10. Red chili powder   -   3 tsp
11. Turmeric powder   -   ½ tsp
12. Fenugreek powder   -   a little
13. Asafetida   -   ¼ tsp

Boil gooseberry in water in a container. Ensure that the gooseberries remain completely submerged in water. Cook till the segments separate. Drain off water and separate the segments. Separate out the seeds. Boil salt in 1 cup water and keep aside. In a wok, sauté ingredients 3 to 6 well. Remove from wok and keep aside.

Sauté gooseberry segments in oil. Separate from oil once sautéed. Now sauté ingredients 10 to 13 in oil well. Add the sautéed ingredients and the gooseberry into the spice mixture. Pour in salt water and mix well.

RAW MANGO CARROT PICKLE

Ingredients

1. Raw mango   -   1 kg
   (cut into thin slices lengthwise)
2. Carrot   -   1 kg
   (cut into thin slices lengthwise)
3. Green chilies   -   15
   (Half slit)
4. Garlic cloves
   (sliced lengthwise into two) -   ½ cup
5. Ginger   -   1 large piece
   (sliced lengthwise as garlic)
6. Curry leaves   -   3 sprigs
7. Water   -   3 cups
8. Salt   -   2 large spoons
9. Vinegar   -   1 large spoon
10. Mustard seeds   -   a little
11. Oil   -   1 large spoon

Boil salt in water and keep aside. Pop mustard seeds in oil and sauté ingredients 3 to 6 well. Once sautéed, keep separately. Into the same oil, sauté mango and carrot slices. Add in the sautéed ingredients and put off the flame. Pour in salt water, vinegar and mix well. Store in a clean and dry container.

LEMON WHITE PICKLE

Ingredients

1. Lemons   -   6
   (washed, wiped, cut into 8 pieces each and deseeded)
2. Green chilies   -   8
   (big & half slit)
3. Garlic cloves   -   12
   (slit lengthwise) (6 needed if large sized)
4. Ginger   -   1
   (medium piece)(sliced lengthwise)
5. Curry leaves   -   1 sprig
6. Shallots (finely chopped)   -   1
7. Mustard seeds   -   ¼ tsp
8. Water   -   ½ cup
9. Cooking oil   -   1½ large spoons
10. Coconut oil   -   1 tsp
11. Vinegar   -   2 tsp
12. Salt   -   1 tsp full.

Boil salt in ½ cup water. Heat coconut oil and crackle mustard seeds followed by chopped shallots. Keep them aside. Further heat oil and sauté ingredients 2, 3 & 4. Once sautéed, add curry leaves. Separate them out. Now add lemon pieces and sauté. Once nicely done, add sautéed ingredients, salt, boiled salt water and vinegar. Mix well. Add crackled mustard seeds and shallots along with coconut oil. Switch off the flame once the contents come to a boil.

CAKE

Ingredients

1.	Maida/ All-purpose flour	-	1 glass
2.	Sugar powdered	-	1 glass
3.	Oil	-	3/4 glass
4.	Eggs	-	4
5.	Sugar (for caramel)	-	1 tbsp
6.	Cashew nuts (halved)	-	20
7.	Raisins	-	50
8.	Tutti Frutti	-	50
9.	Vanilla essence	-	16 drops
10.	Pineapple essence	-	16 drops
11.	a. Green cardamom	-	3
	b. Cloves	-	3
	c. Cinnamon	-	1
12.	Baking powder	-	1 dessert spoon
13.	Water	-	½ cup

Sift maida, baking powder and powdered sugar well. Beat eggs and oil in the blender/ mixer well.   Pour into a mixing bowl. Add in the maida mix into it (in small batches).For preparing caramel, melt sugar. Wait for it to turn brown or dark amber in colour. When it starts to smoke and foam gently, pour in water and bring to a boil. Keep aside. Powder ingredient 11. Mix it to the caramel and add in to the flour mixture. Add in both essence and stir until the batter is smooth.

Grease a baking dish and line with a baking paper. Layer dry fruits at the bottom. Now pour or spoon half of the batter over it. Layer dry fruits over the batter again. Pour in the remaining batter. Finally garnish with the dry fruits on the top too. Preheat the oven. Bake the batter in the oven till the crust is brown in colour. Prick with a needle and if it comes out clean, the cake is done.

VATTAYAPPAM

Ingredients

1. Raw white rice   -   2 cups
2. Cooked rice   -   2 tbsp
3. Coconut grated   -   ½
4. Yeast   -   2 tsp
5. Sugar   -   2 tbsp

Soak rice in water for 8 to 10 hrs. Drain water, wash and grind the rice with ingredients 2, 3, 4 & 5.Cover with a lid and keep aside overnight. Add salt and sugar to the batter the next morning and steam the appam.

Printed in Great Britain
by Amazon

39665532R00036